CLAUDIA
RODEN

FUL MEDAMES AND OTHER VEGETARIAN DISHES

PENGUIN BOOKS

PENGUIN BOOKS

Published by the Penguin Group. Penguin Books Ltd, 27 Wrights Lane, London
w8 5tz, England. Penguin Books USA Inc., 375 Hudson Street, New York,
New York 10014, USA. Penguin Books Australia Ltd, Ringwood, Victoria, Australia.
Penguin Books Canada Ltd, 10 Alcorn Avenue, Toronto, Ontario, Canada m4v 3b2.
Penguin Books (NZ) Ltd, 182–190 Wairau Road, Auckland 10, New Zealand · Penguin
Books Ltd, Registered Offices: Harmondsworth, Middlesex, England · Extracted from
A New Book of Middle Eastern Food by Claudia Roden, first published by Viking
1985. (A revised edition of *A Book of Middle Eastern Food*, Thomas Nelson, 1968.)
Published in Penguin Books 1986. This edition published 1996. Copyright © Claudia
Roden, 1968, 1985. All rights reserved · Typeset by Rowland Phototypesetting Ltd,
Bury St Edmunds, Suffolk. Printed in England by Clays Ltd, St Ives plc · Except
in the United States of America, this book is sold subject to the condition that it
shall not, by way of trade or otherwise, be lent, re-sold, hired out, or otherwise
circulated without the publisher's prior consent in any form of binding or cover other
than that in which it is published and without a similar condition including this
condition being imposed on the subsequent purchaser · 10 9 8 7 6 5 4 3 2 1

CONTENTS

AUBERGINE PURÉE

This way of preparing aubergines, sometimes called 'poor man's caviar', is a favourite all over the Middle East.

3 aubergines
3 tablespoons olive oil
2—3 tablespoons chopped parsley
1—2 cloves garlic, crushed
Juice of 1 lemon, or more
Salt and black pepper

The best way of preparing this purée is to grill the aubergines over charcoal, which gives them a distinctive flavour. However, it will probably be more convenient to grill them under a grill or place them over a gas flame; either way is very successful. Sear them until the skins are black and start to blister, and the flesh feels soft and juicy. Rub the skins off under the cold tap, taking care to remove any charred particles. Gently squeeze out as much of the juice as possible, since it is rather bitter.

Put the aubergines in a bowl and mash them with a fork, or pound them to a smooth paste in a mortar. An electric blender will give excellent results. Add the oil gradually, beating all the time. Then add the remaining ingredients, mixing vigorously to blend them into the purée. Taste and add more lemon juice, garlic or seasonings as you wish.

Serve as an appetizer or salad.

- Many people these days find it easier to roast the aubergines in a very high oven until they soften – instead of grilling. It is a good idea to put 2 small onions in to soften with the aubergines. Chop them up and mix them into the aubergine purée.
- A lovely salad can also be made by stirring into the purée 3 large peeled and chopped tomatoes and a small grated onion.

AUBERGINE SLICES WITH ONIONS AND TOMATOES

This is an elegant buffet version of *Imam Bayildi* (page 45).

> *3 medium-sized aubergines*
> *Salt and pepper*
> *2 onions, coarsely chopped*
> *Olive or a light vegetable oil*
> *2 cloves garlic, crushed*
> *1 large tin peeled tomatoes*
> *A small bunch of parsley, finely chopped*
> *2 tablespoons pine nuts*

Cut the aubergines into 1½-cm (½-inch) slices. Sprinkle generously with salt and let them sweat in a colander for about an hour.

For the filling, fry the onions in 2 tablespoons oil until golden. Add the garlic and stir. When the aroma rises, add the peeled tomatoes with only half their juice. Season to taste with salt and pepper and cook until the liquid is reduced, then stir in the parsley.

Rinse the salt off the aubergines and gently squeeze a few slices at a time together between the palms of your hands to get rid of some of their juices. Deep fry quickly in very hot oil (this so they absorb much less of it), turning over once, until just coloured.

Press on absorbent paper, then arrange on a large serving dish.

Spread a little of the filling over each slice. Toast the pine nuts over low heat in a frying pan with no oil, shaking it until they are lightly browned. Sprinkle them over the filling.

Serve cold.

- Lately, on the advice of a Turkish lady, I have been stewing the aubergine slices in tomato juice with a drop of oil instead of frying them – which is lighter and also very good.

TAHINA CREAM SALAD WITH YOGHOURT

This version has a very definite flavour of its own and is rather creamier than most. My mother discovered it in the Sudan, and has made it ever since.

> *2–3 cloves garlic*
> *Salt*
> *150 ml (¼ pint) tahina paste*
> *150 ml (¼ pint) yoghourt*
> *Juice of 2½ lemons, or more*
> *Finely chopped parsley, to garnish*

Crush the garlic with a little salt and mix it with the tahina paste. Add the yoghourt and lemon juice gradually, beating vigorously to make a smooth, thick cream. Taste and add more salt, lemon juice or garlic if necessary. (Here an electric mixer or blender can be very useful.)

Serve in a bowl, garnished with finely chopped parsley, and provide Arab or other bread to dip into it.

Serve as an appetizer, or to accompany salads.

BABA GHANOUSH (ALSO CALLED MOUTABAL)

Aubergines with Tahina

This rich cream is a combination of two strong flavours: the smoky one of aubergines prepared as below, and the strong taste of tahina sharpened by lemon and garlic. It is exciting and vulgarly seductive. The ingredients are added almost entirely to taste, the harmony of flavours depending largely on the size and flavour of the aubergines used.

The quantities below give a fairly large amount, enough to be served as a dip at a party.

> *3 large aubergines*
> *2–4 cloves garlic, or to taste*
> *Salt*
> *180 ml (¼ pint) tahina paste or less, depending on the size of the aubergines*
> *Juice of 3 lemons, or more to taste*
> *½ teaspoon ground cumin (optional)*
> *2 tablespoons finely chopped parsley*
> *A few black olives or 1 tomato, thinly sliced, to garnish*

Cook the aubergines over charcoal or under a gas or electric grill (or roast them in a hot oven) as described in the recipe for aubergine purée (page 1), until the skin blackens and blisters. Peel and wash the aubergines, and squeeze out as much of the bitter juice as possible.

Crush the garlic cloves with salt. Mash the aubergines with a potato masher or fork, then add the crushed garlic and a little more salt, and pound to a smooth, creamy purée. Alternatively, use an electric blender to make the purée.

Add the tahina paste and lemon juice alternately, beating well or blending for a few seconds between each addition. Taste and add more salt, lemon juice, garlic or tahina if you think it necessary, and if you like, a little cumin.

Pour the cream into a bowl or a few smaller flat serving dishes. Garnish with finely chopped parsley and black olives, or with a few tomato slices. Serve as an appetizer with Arab or other bread, as a salad, or as a party dip.

BOILED CARROT SALAD

This is a fiery Moroccan salad. Make it with old carrots, which taste better. Add the flavourings gradually, to taste. The colour is beautiful. Serve as a dip with bread or bits of raw vegetables.

500 g (1 lb) carrots
Salt and pepper
½–1 teaspoon harissa,1 or 1 teaspoon paprika and a good
 pinch of cayenne
1–2 teaspoons cumin
3 tablespoons wine vinegar
4 tablespoons olive oil
2 cloves garlic, crushed
¼–½ teaspoon ginger
A few olives to garnish

Peel the carrots and boil in salted water until very soft. Drain and mash with a fork in a bowl and stir in the rest of the ingredients or, better still, turn to a smooth purée in a blender.

Serve cold garnished with a few green or black olives.

1A fiery pimento paste. It can be bought ready made.

- Alternative additional flavourings are 2 tablespoons honey and 1 teaspoon cinnamon.

DUKKAH

This is another dearly loved and old Egyptian speciality. It is a loose mixture of nuts and spices in a dry, crushed but not powdered form, usually eaten with bread dipped in olive oil. In Egypt it is served at breakfast time, as an appetizer, or as a snack in the evening. It is a very personal and individual mixture which varies from one family to another. Here are two mixtures, the first is my mother's.

> 500 g (1 lb) sesame seed
> 250 g (8 oz) coriander seed
> 120 g (4 oz) hazelnuts
> 120 g (4 oz) ground cumin
> Salt and pepper to taste – try 1 teaspoon salt and
> ½ teaspoon black pepper

Roast or grill the ingredients separately. Pound them together until they are finely crushed but not pulverized. The crushing can be done in a mincer or an electric blender. In the last case run it for a very short time only, as otherwise the oil from the too finely ground seeds and nuts will form a paste with the pulverized ingredients. *Dukkah* should always be a crushed dry mixture, and definitely not a paste.

The quantities above make a good deal of *dukkah*, but it can be stored for many weeks in covered jars.

6   From a book published in 1860:

A meal is often made by those who cannot afford luxuries of bread and a mixture called *dukkah*, which is commonly composed of salt and pepper with *za'atar* or wild marjoram or mint or cumin-seed, and with one or more, or all, of the following ingredients – namely, coriander seed, cinnamon, sesame, and hummus (or chick peas). Each mouthful of bread is dipped in this mixture.[1]

Try mixing the ingredients to taste and improvise the proportions. Roast or grill the ingredients separately before pounding them. If you use chick peas, buy those sold pre-cooked, salted and dried, available in most Greek and Indian shops. They are tiny, white and very round.

• Another very humble preparation, a mixture of dried crushed mint, salt and pepper, is sold in the streets in little paper cornets as *dukkah* to sprinkle over bread.

TABBOULEH

Parsley and Mint Salad with Burghul (Cracked Wheat)

This very refreshing salad – all green herbs with buff-coloured wheat speckle – has become quite well-known in this country through the recently opened Lebanese restaurants. A mountain dish that became a national dish, it is now popular throughout the world.

This recipe is different from the one in the first edition of this book, which had more wheat and less herbs. That one had been brought back from Aleppo to Egypt by my father's family

1Lane, *Manners and Customs of the Modern Egyptians.*

almost ninety years ago – a time when people needed to fill their stomachs.

Tabbouleh makes a wonderful first course and is always welcome on a buffet table.

> 250–310 g (8–10 oz) parsley (preferably flat-leafed),
>   chopped
> 60–90 g (2–3 oz) fresh mint, chopped
> 60–120 g (2–4 oz) fine ground burghul (cracked wheat)
> Salt and pepper to taste
> Juice of 2 lemons, or more to taste
> 100 ml (3 fl oz) olive oil
> 250 g (8 oz) spring onions or 1 large, mild onion, chopped
> Young Cos lettuce leaves to garnish
> 3 medium tomatoes, diced

Wash the mint and parsley if necessary and dry well. Remove stems and chop (a food processor will do this well, but be careful that you do not turn them to a mush). Soak the burghul in cold water for 10 minutes, drain and press to remove excess water. Put it in a bowl and add salt and pepper and some of the lemon juice and the olive oil. Let it absorb the dressing for about half an hour or until it is tender. Just before serving, add the burghul to the chopped parsley, a little at a time, just enough for a speckled effect. Add the spring onions, seasonings and more dressing to taste and mix well. The salad should be distinctly sharp with lavish quantities of lemon.

Serve on a large, flat plate or individual small ones, surrounded if you like by the pale crisp leaves from the heart of Cos lettuce to be used as a scoop. (In the mountain villages of Lebanon, freshly picked, sharp young vine leaves are passed around to pick up the salad.) Top with the chopped tomatoes.

BAZARGAN

This old recipe from Aleppo in Syria was rediscovered by my parents in Los Angeles. Quantities are enough for at least fifteen people but the salad keeps well if you have some left over.

500 g (1 lb) burghul (cracked wheat)
2 large onions, grated or finely chopped
150 ml (¼ pint) olive oil (you may use sunflower oil)
250 g (8 oz) tomato concentrate
2 tablespoons oregano
60 g (2 oz) finely chopped parsley
120 g (4 oz) walnuts, coarsely chopped
3 tablespoons concentrated pomegranate juice or the juice
  of 2 lemons
2 teaspoons cumin
2 teaspoons coriander
1 teaspoon allspice
Salt and pepper to taste
Cayenne pepper to taste

Wash and soak the burghul in fresh cold water for 10 to 15 minutes. Drain well through a fine sieve. Soften the onions by frying in a little of the oil but do not brown.

Mix all the ingredients very thoroughly with a fork in a large bowl. Leave for a few hours, preferably overnight, in the refrigerator, for the burghul to absorb all the flavours and to become tender.

SWEET PEPPER SALAD

3 sweet green peppers
1 tablespoon finely chopped parsley

Dressing

1 tablespoon lemon juice or vinegar, or more
3 tablespoons olive oil
1–2 cloves garlic, crushed (optional)
Salt and black pepper

Cut the peppers in half and taste a small piece from each one in case it is too strong. Remove the seeds and grill the peppers under a low flame until their skins blister and darken, and their flesh becomes soft. Skin them, and cut them into long strips. Crisp and sharp when raw, they become mellow and sweet when grilled.

Put the peppers in a serving bowl. Mix the dressing ingredients together, using either salad oil or olive oil. Stir in parsley, pour over the peppers and mix well.

PIAZ

Turkish Haricot Bean Salad

120 g (4 oz) dried haricot beans, soaked overnight
4 tablespoons olive oil
Juice of ½ lemon, or more
Salt and black pepper

2 hard-boiled eggs
4 black olives
1 tomato, thinly sliced

Boil the beans until very tender and soft, bearing in mind their age and quality in assessing the cooking time. Take care not to overcook them if using a pressure cooker. They must be firm.

Drain the beans well. While still hot, add the olive oil, lemon juice, salt and pepper. Mix in the eggs cut into eighths, the black olives, pitted and halved, and thinly sliced tomato, taking care not to crumble or crush them, or the beans.

LEEKS WITH LEMON AND SUGAR

This is a particularly delicious sweet-and-sour way of preparing leeks.

1 kg (2 lb) leeks
2–3 cloves garlic, crushed
1 tablespoon sugar
3–4 tablespoons sunflower oil
Juice of 1–2 lemons

Wash the leeks carefully, removing any soil nestling between the leaves. Cut off the tough green part of the leaves. Cut the rest into medium pieces.

Fry the garlic and sugar in hot oil until the sugar becomes slightly caramelized. Add the leeks and turn them a little over a moderate heat to colour them lightly. Sprinkle with lemon juice. Stew gently, covered, in this and the vegetables' own juices over very low heat until tender.

Serve hot or cold.

TARTOUFA IN TOMATO SAUCE

1 kg (2¼ lb) Jerusalem artichokes
1 onion, finely chopped
1 clove garlic, halved
3 tablespoons olive oil
3 tomatoes, skinned and chopped
2 tablespoons tomato concentrate
2 tablespoons finely chopped parsley
Salt and black pepper
Juice of ½ lemon (optional)

Wash and peel the artichokes. Fry the onion and garlic in olive oil until soft and golden. Add the artichokes and roll them in the oil by shaking the pan. Add the tomatoes and squash them into the oil. Add tomato concentrate, parsley, seasoning, and lemon juice if used. Stir well and cover with water. Simmer gently for half an hour, or until the artichokes are tender and the sauce is rich and reduced. Add more water during cooking if necessary.

SALATA HORIATIKI

Greek Country Salad

This salad brings back for me the garland of islands floating in the deep blue sea, the plaintive sound of the bouzouki and the sugar-cake houses. It can serve as a meal.

1 Cos lettuce, cut into ribbons
2 large knobbly tomatoes, cut in wedges

1 cucumber, not necessarily peeled, split in half through
  its length and cut into thick slices
1 green pepper, cut in thin rings crosswise
1 large mild onion, thinly sliced and the rings separated,
  or a bunch of spring onions, thinly sliced
250 g (8 oz) Feta cheese, cut into small squares or
  broken with your fingers into coarse pieces
1 dozen or more black Kalamata olives
A good bunch of parsley, preferably the flat-leafed type,
  coarsely chopped

Dressing
90 ml (6 tablespoons) olive oil
Juice of 1 lemon
Salt and pepper

Put all the salad ingredients together in a large bowl. Just before serving, mix the dressing to taste, beat well, pour over the salad and toss.

- Other usual additions are chopped dill or fennel, capers, sliced pickled gherkin, a sprinkling of oregano, a few sprigs of fresh mint, finely chopped.

CACIK

Cucumber and Yoghourt Salad

A Turkish salad makes an extremely popular *mezze* throughout the Middle East. It is sometimes served as a cold soup.

1 large cucumber or 2 small ones, peeled and diced
Salt
2–3 cloves garlic
450 ml (¾ pint) yoghourt
White pepper
1 tablespoon dried crushed mint or 3 tablespoons finely
   chopped fresh mint, or to taste
Additional mint, to garnish

Sprinkle the diced cucumber with salt, and leave in a colander to drain for half an hour. Crush the garlic with a little salt; use more than 3 cloves if you like. Mix a few tablespoons of the yoghourt with the garlic, then add the mixture to the rest of the yoghourt and mix well. Add more salt and pepper to taste. Finally add the mint, whose aroma and flavour make the salad deliciously refreshing. Drain the cucumbers and mix with the yoghourt.

Pour into a serving dish and decorate with more mint.

• For a sharper flavour you may stir in 2 tablespoons vinegar and 4 of olive oil.
• Another lovely alternative is to use a mixture of sour cream and yoghourt in equal quantities.

MICHOTETA

Cream Cheese and Cucumber Salad

This delightful Egyptian salad is usually made with salty Greek cream cheese, either Teleme or Feta. For an authentic salad, these can be found in most Greek stores, but good-quality cottage or curd cheese makes a good substitute.

> *250 g (8 oz) soft cheese (see above)*
> *Juice of 1 lemon*
> *2 tablespoons olive oil*
> *1 red Italian or large mild onion, finely chopped*
> *½ large cucumber, peeled and diced*
> *Salt and black pepper*

Crumble the cheese with a tablespoon of water, using a fork, and work in the lemon juice and olive oil. Mix in the onion and cucumber, and season with salt and pepper (Feta does not need salt).

This salad is wonderful as an appetizer or as an accompaniment to the dish of brown beans called *ful medames* (page 34).

SPINACH SALAD WITH YOGHOURT

Spinach has a remarkable affinity with yoghourt, and it is delicious prepared in this particular manner.

> *500 g (1 lb) fresh spinach or 250 g (8 oz) frozen leaf*
>   *spinach*
> *150 ml (¼ pint) yoghourt*
> *1 clove garlic, crushed*
> *Salt and black pepper*

Wash the spinach carefully, snipping off any hard stems. Drain. Chop the leaves and stew them in their own juice in a large covered saucepan until tender, about 15 minutes. If using frozen spinach, de-frost it in a colander and simmer until cooked. Allow to cool.

Beat the yoghourt and garlic together, and add the mixture to the pan. Mix well and season to taste with salt and pepper.

LABANEYA

Spinach Soup with Yoghourt

An Egyptian soup traditionally made with the leaves of a plant of the spinach family called *silq* (beet); the French call it *blette*. The soup is equally delicious made with spinach, fresh if possible, but frozen leaf spinach will also do. (I often find *silq* in Greek stores.)

> *500 g (1 lb) silq (beet) or fresh spinach, or 250 g (8 oz)*
> *   frozen leaf spinach*
> *1 onion*
> *About 2 tablespoons oil*
> *1 leek or 3–4 spring onions, finely chopped*
> *120 g (4 oz) rice*
> *Salt and black pepper*
> *500 ml (¾ pint) yoghourt*
> *1 clove garlic, or more, crushed*
> *½ teaspoon turmeric (optional)*

Wash the beets or fresh spinach leaves in a bowlful of water. Drain and cut into large pieces or ribbons, but do not chop them.

Chop the onion and sauté in oil in a large saucepan until faintly coloured and soft. Add the spinach, stir and sauté gently. A finely chopped leek or a few spring onions will add a delicate flavour to the soup. Add them to the saucepan, together with the washed and drained rice. Cover with 1 litre (2 pints) water, season with salt and pepper, bring to the boil and simmer gently until the rice and spinach are cooked. This will take about 15 minutes, and the rice should not be allowed to get too soft or mushy.

In the meantime, beat the yoghurt with one or more crushed cloves of garlic. When the rice and spinach are ready, add the yoghurt mixture to the soup and beat well. Heat but do not let the soup boil again, or it will curdle.

A pinch of turmeric added to the spinach and rice while they are cooking will give the soup a pale yellow, Oriental tinge.

SWEET-AND-SOUR ONIONS

500 g (1 lb) little button onions
3–4 tablespoons olive oil
3 tablespoons wine vinegar
1 tablespoon sugar
2 tablespoons sultanas
Salt and pepper
2 teaspoons dried mint (optional)

Peel the onions (one way is to plunge them for a few seconds in boiling water until the skins come off easily). Sauté in oil, shaking the pan to brown them all over. Add the rest of the ingredients and a little water and cook gently till soft, adding more water if necessary.

COURGETTES WITH RAISINS AND PINE NUTS

Slice 500 g (1 lb) courgettes and fry quickly in 3–4 tablespoons olive oil with 2 tablespoons raisins or sultanas and 2 tablespoons pine nuts. Add 1 crushed clove garlic, salt and pepper, and 2 teaspoons dried mint (optional) and stir well. Squeeze the juice of ½ lemon, or more, over the salad and serve cold.

- Lately I have not fried the courgettes but macerated them in a lemon vinaigrette for at least an hour. It is healthier and delicious, but the courgettes must be very good and tasty. Toast the pine nuts and add them before serving. This is best without garlic.

BAMIA

Sweet-and-Sour Okra

A slight sweet-and-sour flavour is particularly good with cold dishes.

Cut off the stem ends and wash 500 g (1 lb) small young okra. Heat 2 tablespoons oil in a heavy pan. Add the okra and sauté gently for about 5 minutes. Turn each pod over, then stir in 1 tablespoon sugar, salt and pepper, and the juice of 1 small lemon. Add a little water to half-cover the okra.

Simmer, covered, for about 20 minutes or longer, adding a little water occasionally if necessary, and cook until tender. Allow to cool before serving.

LENTIL AND TOMATO SALAD

250 g (8 oz) large brown lentils
1 large onion, chopped
4 tablespoons olive oil
3 tomatoes, peeled and cut into pieces
Salt and pepper
1 small bunch of parsley, finely chopped
2–3 tablespoons vinegar

Soak the lentils in water for a few hours. Fry the onion in oil until lightly coloured. Add the tomatoes and sauté for a minute. Add the drained lentils, cover with water and simmer gently for about ½ hour until they are tender, adding water as required, then season with salt and pepper, add parsley and vinegar and cook until the lentils are done and the liquid absorbed.

Taste and adjust the seasoning when it is cool. You may add a sprinkling of olive oil if you like.

FUL NABED

Purée of Dried White Broad Beans

Choose the white broad beans to be found in all Greek shops and some delicatessens, usually skinned.

> *2 onions, finely chopped*
> *6 tablespoons olive oil*
> *250 g (8 oz) dried white broad beans, soaked overnight*
> *Juice of 1 lemon*
> *1 teaspoon caster sugar*
> *Salt*

Dressing

> *2 tablespoons olive oil*
> *Juice of ½ lemon*
> *2–3 tablespoons finely chopped fresh dill or parsley*
> *1 teaspoon paprika or a pinch of cayenne pepper (optional)*

Fry the onions gently in oil in a large saucepan until they are only just soft and a very pale golden colour. Add about ½ litre (¾ pint) 19 water and bring to the boil. Drain the beans of their soaking water, add them to the saucepan, and cook over low heat without any salt until they practically disintegrate. Add more water during the cooking time if necessary. This will take from 1 to 1½ hours, according to the quality of the beans.

When the beans are ready, there should be hardly any liquid left. Mash them to a paste. Season with the lemon juice, sugar and salt. For a very creamy consistency put the mixture through a sieve or in an electric blender.

Pour the purée into a serving bowl. When cold, decorate with a dribble of olive oil, lemon juice and chopped dill or parsley. Red paprika may be added to this mixture for colour, or cayenne pepper for strength.

CHAKCHOUKA

This is a dish of Tunisian origin which today is eaten in most Middle Eastern countries. A Turkish version is called *menemen*.

> *1 – 3 green peppers, depending on size*
> *2 onions*
> *8 small tomatoes*
> *Butter or olive oil*
> *Salt and black pepper*
> *6 eggs*

Cut the peppers open and remove the cores and seeds. Cut them into strips. Slice the onions and cut the tomatoes in half.

Fry the onions and peppers in butter or oil in a large frying pan. Season to taste with salt and pepper, and let them stew gently in their own juices. When the peppers are soft, add the halved tomatoes and continue cooking until they, too, are soft. Taste the mixture, adding more seasoning if necessary. Drop the eggs in whole, and cook until set. Season again if necessary, and serve.

In some versions, the eggs are not left whole but stirred and blended with the vegetables to achieve a creamy texture.

Variations

1. Fry 4 sliced courgettes or 1 cubed aubergine at the same time as the onions and peppers.
2. Add 3 medium-sized cooked potatoes, cut into pieces.
3. For alternative flavourings fry 2 crushed cloves garlic with 2 tablespoons dried mint. Add a sprinkling of paprika or make it fiery with a teaspoon of *harissa* (see footnote page 5) or a good pinch of cayenne.

SANBUSAK

Here is a modern recipe for *sanbusak*, popular in Syria, the Lebanon and Egypt. The recipe for the dough has for centuries been explained as 'one coffee cup of oil, one coffee cup of melted butter, one coffee cup of warm water, one teaspoon of salt. Add and work in as much flour as it takes.' Translated into English weights and measures, it is:

Dough

120 ml (4 fl oz) oil
120 g (4 oz) butter, melted
120 ml (4 fl oz) warm water
1 teaspoon salt

500 g (1 lb) plain flour, sifted
Cheese Spinach or Aubergine Filling (see below)
1 egg, beaten
Sesame seeds (optional)
Clarified butter for shallow-frying or oil for deep-frying

To make the dough: put the oil and butter together in a small heatproof bowl, and heat over boiling water until the butter has melted. Mix with warm water and salt, and pour into a large mixing bowl.

Add flour gradually, stirring slowly with a knife and then your hand, until the dough forms a soft, rather greasy ball. A few tablespoons more flour may be required. The dough should be handled as little as possible, so stop mixing as soon as it holds together.

Traditionally, *sanbusak* are half-moon-shaped. Either roll the dough out thinly on a floured board and cut into rounds about 8 cm (3 inches) in diameter with a pastry cutter, or take walnut-sized lumps and flatten them out as thinly as possible between the palms of your hands.

Put a heaped teaspoonful of filling in the centre of one half of each circle. Fold the other half over to make a half-moon shape and seal by pinching the edges tightly. If you like, make the traditional festoon-type edge by pinching and folding over all along. Arrange on baking sheets, which need not be greased.

Brush the surface with beaten egg and, if you like, sprinkle lightly with sesame seeds. Bake in a preheated slow to moderate oven (160°–180°C/350°–375°F/Mark 3–4) until they are a pale golden colour, about 35 to 45 minutes. Alternatively, fry gently in clarified butter until golden and well cooked inside, which takes only a few minutes, or deep-fry in oil. In this case, do not brush with the egg and water mixture.

Serve hot or cold, but preferably just out of the oven, when they are at their best. Depending on the size of the *sanbusak*, this quantity makes about 30 pastries.

• Here is a similar alternative dough: Work the oil and creamed butter into the flour, and add milk instead of water gradually until the dough becomes a ball and leaves the sides of the bowl. In this case, too, do not work the dough longer than necessary.

SAVOURY FILLINGS

Cheese Filling

*500 g (1 lb) crumbly white Greek Feta cheese or about
  equal quantities of Feta and cottage cheese
3–4 tablespoons finely chopped fresh parsley, dill, mint or
  chives
White pepper*

Crumble the cheese with a fork. Do not use a cream cheese because it melts. Mix in chopped herbs and season to taste with white pepper, but do not add salt unless the cheese requires it. (Feta is very salty.) Work the ingredients into a paste.

Spinach Filling

*500 g (1 lb) fresh spinach or 250 g (8 oz) frozen chopped
  or leaf spinach
1 tablespoon butter
120 g (4 oz) Gruyère, Cheddar or Wensleydale cheese, grated*

1 egg
Black pepper
¼ teaspoon grated nutmeg (optional)

Trim stems of fresh spinach; wash carefully and chop the leaves finely. Put in a pan with a tablespoon of butter. Cover and let it cook in its own juice over very low heat, stirring occasionally, until tender. If using frozen spinach, de-frost it and squeeze all the water out.

Stir in the grated cheese, the lightly beaten egg, and black pepper to taste. Do not add salt unless necessary. Take into account the saltiness of the cheese melting into the spinach. Add a little nutmeg if you like, and mix well.

Khandrajo (Aubergine) Filling

This is a Sephardic Jewish filling similar to the French *ratatouille*.

500 g (1 lb) unpeeled aubergines, cut into small cubes
Salt
Oil
1 large onion, finely chopped
3 tomatoes, skinned and chopped
Black pepper

Sprinkle cubed aubergines with salt and leave them in a colander for about half an hour to allow the bitter juices to drain away. Rinse well and squeeze lightly.

Heat 2 tablespoons oil in a saucepan and fry the chopped onion to a dark golden colour. Add the aubergines and fry lightly until tender and a little coloured. Add the tomatoes and season generously with pepper. Add salt only if required, taking into account the aubergines, which are salty already. Simmer gently, covered, until the vegetables are very soft, then squash them lightly with a fork.

EGGAH

I have classed the *eggah* as an egg dish or omelette, but this is misleading unless one describes its character further. The idea of an omelette, influenced by the image of the French version, implies extreme lightness, softness, creaminess and a slight fluidity in texture. If one looked for these qualities in an Arab *eggah*, one could well feel disappointed.

An *eggah* is firm and sound, rather like an egg cake. It is usually 2 cm (1 inch) or more thick, and generally bursting with a filling of vegetables, suspended like currants in a cake. The egg is used as a binding for the filling, rather than the filling being an adornment of the egg. For serving, the *eggah* is turned out on to a serving dish and cut into slices, as one would cut a cake. It is sometimes cooked in a rectangular dish, especially if baked in the oven. In this case, it is usually served cut into rectangular or square pieces.

These extremely popular dishes are used for several purposes. They are cut into very small pieces as hors d'œuvre or into larger ones as first courses, and they are also used as side dishes to accompany more substantial dishes.

An *eggah* can be eaten cold as well as hot, which makes it a good luncheon or party piece. It is a great favourite for picnics and pilgrimages during national holidays. The fact that a very large one can be prepared to serve several people, cooked in advance and warmed up or eaten cold, gives it a great advantage over the French type of omelette, which must be small, and eaten immediately it is prepared to be successful.

As far as the pan is concerned, any large heavy frying pan which will assure an even distribution of heat can be used. One with its own lid, or any lid or plate which fits it tightly, is useful. If the dish is to be baked in the oven, any ovenproof dish will do, provided it has a lid.

When the dish is cooked on top of the stove, it requires from 15 to 30 minutes over very gentle heat, according to the number of eggs used and the type of filling, and depending on whether the filling has been cooked beforehand. It is usually cooked covered.

If it is cooked in the oven, the tray or dish must first be greased with butter. The cooking time in a 160°C (325°F/Mark 3) oven varies from half an hour to 1 hour, again depending on the size of the dish and the type of filling. The dish may be covered to begin with, and then uncovered towards the end to allow the top to brown. When cooked, the *eggah* should be firm, even in the centre.

I prefer the first method over heat.

Butter or *samna* (clarified butter) is commonly used to cook these omelettes but oil will also do.

In Persia, the *eggah* is called a *kuku*, and plays a particularly impressive role in the cuisine. It is served on almost all occasions, as an appetizer, a first course or a side dish.

These omelettes can be turned into small fritters (tiny *eggahs*) by dropping the egg mixture by the tablespoon into a little hot oil in a frying pan and turning them over to brown on the other side. They are usually as good hot as they are cold and make tasty party finger foods.

EGGAH BI KORRAT

Leek Eggah

750 g (1½ lb) leeks
Butter
½ teaspoon sugar
Juice of ½ lemon
Salt and black pepper
6 eggs

Wash the leeks, trimming off the roots and removing the outer leaves. Cut off the tough tops of the leaves and wash the leeks again carefully. Cut into thinnish slices. Sauté in a little butter, then season with the sugar, lemon juice, and salt and pepper to taste. Let the leeks stew in their own juices until soft and lightly coloured.

Alternatively, the leeks can be washed and trimmed as above, then boiled in salted water until just soft, drained and chopped.

Beat the eggs lightly in a large bowl. Add the leek mixture, mix again and adjust seasoning. Cook as usual, in a frying pan or in the oven, and serve cut in slices.

EGGAH BI SABANEH

Spinach Eggah

500 g (1 lb) fresh spinach or 250 g (8 oz) frozen leaf
  spinach
6 eggs

Salt and black pepper
Pinch of nutmeg
Butter

Wash spinach thoroughly, if fresh. Stew it in its own juice until tender. Drain well and chop. If you are using frozen spinach, allow to de-frost, then drain it thoroughly and simmer in its own juice until tender.

Beat the eggs and add the chopped spinach. Mix well, and season with salt, pepper and nutmeg. Cook as usual, in a frying pan or in the oven.

Turn out on to a heated serving dish, and serve cut in slices like a cake. Accompany with yoghourt and a salad if serving it as a main dish.

KUKUYE SABSI

The Persian *eggah*-type omelettes called *kuku* are generally baked in the oven. *Kukuye sabsi* is particularly Persian in flavour and texture. It is made with fresh green herbs and green vegetables, and sometimes with chopped walnuts and raisins.

This is a traditional Iranian New Year's Day dish. Its greenness is believed to be a symbol of fruitfulness in the coming year, bringing prosperity and happiness.

Any favoured herbs may be used in addition to the usual parsley, spring onions, spinach and leeks. (One may use either or both of the last two.) Dill, chervil, tarragon, chives and fresh coriander are others. A few chopped walnuts may be included to add to the quality of the texture and flavour.

2 leeks
120 g (4 oz) spinach
4–5 spring onions
6–8 eggs
2–3 tablespoons chopped parsley
3 tablespoons mixed chopped fresh herbs
2 tablespoons walnuts, chopped (optional)
2 tablespoons raisins (optional)
Salt and black pepper
2 tablespoons softened butter

Wash the vegetables, dry them and chop them very finely. Beat the eggs in a large bowl, add the chopped vegetables, parsley and mixed herbs, and a few chopped walnuts or raisins if liked. Season to taste with salt and pepper, and mix well.

Butter an ovenproof dish and pour in the egg mixture. Bake in a slow oven (160°C/325°F/Mark 3) for 45 minutes, covering the dish for the first 30 minutes. The vegetables should be tender and the eggs set, with a golden crust on top. Alternatively, cook the *kuku* in a large frying pan like an *eggah*. When the eggs have almost set, brown the *kuku* under a hot grill or turn out on a plate and slip back into the pan to colour the underside.

Serve hot or cold as an appetizer or side dish, accompanied by yoghourt.

CHICK PEAS, BEANS AND LENTILS

Since ancient times, dishes based on chick peas, beans, lentils and cereals have been looked down on as the food of the poor. In literature, proverbs and songs they are constantly referred to as 'the food of the poor' or 'the food of the mean'. They have even been included as such in the *Kitab al Buhala* (*Book of Misers*).1

Regardless of this stigma, these dishes are nevertheless loved by rich and poor alike. Numerous jokes are told about Arab dignitaries who, when served with French *haute cuisine* or cosmopolitan food in hotels or at banquets, long for the *ful medames* (page 34) or chick peas and spinach which they can tell that the servants are eating from the aromas wafting up from the kitchens.

A little dull at times, but more often rich and splendidly vulgar, seasoned with spices, garlic, onions and herbs, or used in exciting combinations with other ingredients, pulses are also important for their nutritive value. By themselves, they can be eaten cold as salads or hot as vegetables. Cooked with vegetables, rice and pasta, they add body and texture to many dishes.

Generally, pulses have to be washed and picked clean of impurities, although the majority of the packaged varieties available in Britain are already prepared and quite clean. Most, however, need soaking in cold water for a number of hours, except for the small yellow and red lentils, which cook and disintegrate very quickly. The soaking helps to tenderize the dried vegetables and shorten their cooking time. With brown and green lentils and yellow split peas, soaking helps to shorten this time only slightly. Haricot beans and dried broad white or brown beans require lengthy soaking, but again, some varieties are pre-treated and need only be cooked. When soaking pulses, cover them with a large quantity of cold water since they will quickly swell and absorb a great deal of it.

The time required to cook each variety varies widely according to the soil in which they were grown and their age since drying. However, varieties are constantly being improved and it seems that

1By Jahiz, Damascus, 1938.

each new season's production requires less cooking time than the last.

Always cook in fresh, cold water. Generally, brown and green lentils take between 20 and 40 minutes to become tender. Haricot beans may take any time between 1½ and 3 hours. Black-eyed beans can take as little as 20 minutes. Egyptian brown beans require longer soaking than the others and very long, slow simmering.

Haricot beans, broad white and brown beans must not be salted at the start of cooking, or they will never become soft. They must be seasoned only when already tender.

Dried vegetables can also be pressure-cooked but there is always the danger of over-cooking since the exact time is so often a matter of guesswork, and you may end up with a purée – except in the case of chick peas and yellow split peas, which never disintegrate. Unless pressed for time, therefore, it is preferable not to use this method. It is far better to cook them in advance to ensure that they are ready when needed, since they keep and reheat well.

LENTIL AND VEGETABLE STEW

250 g (8 oz) lentils, soaked overnight if necessary
2 medium potatoes, peeled and coarsely diced
250 g (8 oz) courgettes or marrow, sliced or cubed
250 g (8 oz) leeks, trimmed and sliced
1 stalk celery, sliced
Salt and black pepper
1 onion, finely chopped
Oil
2 cloves garlic, crushed
2 tablespoons finely chopped parsley

Juice of 2 lemons

Drain soaked lentils and simmer in a large pan in 1 pint water for about 20 minutes, or until nearly soft. Add the potatoes, courgettes, leeks and celery, season to taste with salt and pepper, and continue cooking for 15 to 20 minutes longer, or until the vegetables are cooked, adding more water if necessary. Only a little liquid should be left at the end of cooking.

Fry the onion in oil until soft and golden. Add garlic and fry for a minute or two longer until coloured. Drain and add to the lentils and vegetables, together with parsley and lemon juice. Simmer for a few minutes longer, adjust seasoning and serve hot or cold.

LENTILS WITH RISHTA (NOODLES)

250–375 g (8–12 oz) brown or green lentils
Salt
2 onions, finely chopped
Oil
2–3 cloves garlic, crushed
1 teaspoon ground coriander
Black pepper
375 g (12 oz) rishta, noodles or tagliatelle
2 tablespoons butter

Soak lentils and drain. Boil in a fresh portion of salted water to cover (about 600 ml or 1 pint) for between 20 and 30 minutes or until the lentils are soft and the water has been absorbed. Use a large pan which will accommodate the noodles as well. Drain the cooked lentils thoroughly.

Fry the onions in 2 tablespoons oil until soft and golden. Add the garlic and coriander, and continue to fry gently for about 2 minutes, until golden. Add this mixture to the cooked lentils, and season to taste with salt and pepper. Throw the noodles into boiling salted water and cook until just tender (about 10 minutes if using the dried commercial variety). Drain well and add to the lentils. Stir in butter and mix well.

Serve very hot.

• You may also use red lentils for this dish and let them disintegrate to a purée.

FATTA

A number of Arab dishes go under the name of *fatta*, which describes the manner of breaking crisp bread into pieces with your hands. They all have a bed of toasted bread soaked in liquid and a topping of yoghourt with a variety of fillings. The most common filling is chick peas.

All are part of the repertoire which is considered family food because it is filling, and they are not usually given to guests, but in reality they are much more popular than most party dishes.

Pitta bread is opened out, left for a few minutes in a very hot oven or turned under the grill to become crisp and brown, then crumpled into bits in the hand.

Yoghourt is thickened to the consistency of mayonnaise by draining it through muslin in a colander. The usual garnish is fried pine nuts.

FUL MEDAMES

Egyptian Brown Beans

An Egyptian dish which has become 'the' national dish. *Ful medames* is pre-Ottoman and pre-Islamic, claimed by the Copts and probably as old as the Pharaohs. According to an Arab saying: 'Beans have satisfied even the Pharaohs.'

Although basically a peasant dish, the rich and the middle classes also delight in these small dark beans.

Ful medames is eaten in the fields and in village mud houses, in luxury restaurants and on town terraces by masters and servants alike. It is sold in the streets, sometimes buried in Arab bread, garnished with tahina salad and accompanied by a tomato and onion salad. It is the usual substantial breakfast traditionally cooked overnight in an earthen vessel buried up to the neck in ashes or left on the lowest flame of a primus stove.

The small brown beans can be bought in all Greek stores and some delicatessens. Ready-cooked, tinned beans can also be found.

> *1 kg (2 lb) ful medames, soaked overnight*
> *2–4 cloves garlic, crushed (optional)*
> *Finely chopped parsley*
> *Olive oil*
> *Quartered lemons*
> *Salt and freshly ground black pepper*
> *1 teaspoon cumin (optional)*

Boil the soaked beans in a fresh portion of unsalted water in a large saucepan until tender. In the past this took at least 7 hours but the qualities available now are soft after 2 to 2½ hours of gentle sim-

34

mering. A pressure cooker will reduce the time considerably – to 30 or 45 minutes – but care must be taken not to overcook the beans.

When the beans are soft and the liquid reduced, drain them and add crushed garlic to taste, or instead pass some round with the other garnishes for people to take as much as they want.

Serve in soup bowls and sprinkle with chopped parsley. Pass round olive oil, quartered lemons, salt, black pepper and cumin for each person to season as he wishes.

- A pleasant way of thickening the sauce is to throw a handful of red lentils into the water at the start of the cooking.
- In Iraq large brown beans are used instead of the small Egyptian ones in a dish called *badkila*, which also serves for breakfast in the street.
- It is common to serve *hamine* eggs.[1] Put one of these, or a hard-boiled egg, on top of the beans.
- Another way of serving *ful medames* is to smother it in a tomato sauce flavoured with garlic.
- Yet another is to top it with a chopped mixed salad and thinly sliced onions or spring onions.

HARICOT BEANS WITH ONIONS AND TOMATOES

375 g (12 oz) haricot beans, soaked overnight
2 onions, sliced
2 tablespoons oil
2 cloves garlic, sliced

1Eggs simmered very slowly in water containing onion skins.

> 2 tomatoes, skinned and chopped
> 3 tablespoons tomato concentrate
> Salt
> 1 teaspoon paprika
> Pinch of cayenne
> 1 bay leaf
> 2 tablespoons finely chopped parsley (optional)

Drain the soaked beans and boil them in a fresh portion of unsalted water to cover until almost tender. The time will vary from 1 to 2 hours, depending on their age and quality.

Fry the sliced onions in oil until soft and golden. Add garlic and fry for 2 minutes longer. Then add tomatoes and sauté gently until well cooked and almost reduced to a pulp. Stir in tomato concentrate and add the beans, together with some of their cooking water (about 150 ml or ¼ pint). Season to taste with salt, paprika and cayenne. Add a bay leaf and a little chopped parsley if liked.

Mix well and simmer for 15 to 20 minutes longer, until the beans are very soft and coloured a faint salmon pink. Serve hot or cold.

HARIRA

Moroccan Soup

During the thirty days of the fast of Ramadan, every household prepares its own version of this national soup. The smell permeates the streets of Morocco long before sunset, when it is time to break the fast.

This makes enough for 10 to 20 people.

250 g (8 oz) chick peas
250 g (8 oz) haricot beans or other beans
250 g (8 oz) lentils
1 large tin peeled tomatoes
500 g (1 lb) onions, coarsely chopped
Salt and pepper to taste
1 tablespoon turmeric, or to taste
Juice of 1 large lemon, or more
3–4 tablespoons flour
1 small bunch fresh coriander, finely chopped
1 small bunch parsley, finely chopped
120 g (4 oz) cooked rice (optional)
1 teaspoon harissa (optional)

Wash and soak the chick peas, beans and lentils for a few hours or overnight. Drain. Bring the first two to the boil in fresh cold water in a large pan and simmer until tender. Add the lentils and continue to cook until these are just tender. Add the tomatoes, cutting them up into small pieces, the onions and more water. Season to taste with salt and pepper, add turmeric (some people use saffron instead) and lemon juice and simmer a further half hour.

In a small pan stir 600 ml (1 pint) cold water gradually into the flour, beating constantly so as not to have any lumps. Add some strained liquid from the hot soup and stir over low heat until it begins to boil. The flour gives the soup a velvety texture much loved in Morocco. Add the chopped coriander and parsley leaves and pour back into the soup.

Continue to cook until the pulses are soft and the taste is rich. Adjust the seasoning and add water if necessary. Add the rice just before serving and *harissa* (see footnote page 5) if you like.

BAKED RISHTA (NOODLES) WITH AUBERGINES

> *3 large aubergines, sliced*
> *Salt*
> *1 onion, finely chopped*
> *Oil*
> *A 400-g (14-oz) tin skinned tomatoes*
> *1 teaspoon dried oregano*
> *Black pepper*
> *750 g (1½ lb) rishta or spaghetti*
> *Butter*
> *4 hard-boiled eggs, thinly sliced*
> *60 g (2 oz) grated Parmesan*

Sprinkle the aubergine slices with salt and leave them in a colander for at least half an hour to allow the bitter juices to drain away.

Prepare a tomato sauce in the following manner. Fry the onion in 2 tablespoons oil until soft and golden. Add tomatoes and oregano, and season to taste with salt and pepper. Moisten with a little water and simmer, covered, for at least half an hour.

Drain the aubergine slices and pat them dry. Fry them in a little oil until very tender, turning them once. Drain on absorbent paper.

Cook the pasta in vigorously boiling salted water until *al dente* – just tender. Drain, mix with the tomato sauce and 2 tablespoons butter.

Butter a large oven tray or dish. Spread a layer of pasta and sauce over the bottom of the dish; cover with a layer of fried aubergines and one of thinly sliced hard-boiled eggs, and sprinkle with a quarter of the grated Parmesan. Repeat all the layers twice more, so that there are three sets of layers in all. Cover with a thin layer of pasta and sprinkle with the remaining cheese.

Bake in a moderate oven (180°C/350°F/Mark 4) for about 30 minutes, or until a warm golden colour on top.

This dish can be prepared a day ahead and baked just before serving.

MEGADARRA

Here is a modern version of a medieval dish called *mujadarra*, described by al-Baghdadi as a dish of the poor, and still known today as Esau's favourite. In fact, it is such a great favourite that, although said to be for misers, it is a compliment to serve it.

An aunt of mine used to present it regularly to guests with the comment: 'Excuse the food of the poor!' – to which the unanimous reply always was: 'Keep your food of kings and give us *megadarra* every day!'

The proportions of lentils and rice vary with every family. The caramelized onions are the main feature. With the olive oil they are also the main flavouring. In the Lebanon they call it *mudardara*.

> *250 g (8 oz) large brown lentils*
> *2 onions, finely chopped*
> *125 ml (4 fl oz) olive oil*
> *Salt and black pepper*
> *250 g (8 oz) long-grain rice, washed*
> *2–3 onions, sliced into half-moon shapes*

Wash and drain the lentils. Boil in a fresh portion of water to cover for about 25 minutes or until only just tender. Fry the chopped onions in 2 to 3 tablespoons oil until they are brown. Add them to the lentils and season to taste with salt and pepper. Mix well and add rice, together with enough water to make the liquid in the pan up to the volume of rice. Season again and simmer gently, covered, for about 20 minutes until the rice is soft and well cooked, adding a little more water if it becomes absorbed too quickly.

Fry the sliced onions in the rest of the very hot oil until they are dark brown and sweet, almost caramelized.

Serve the rice and lentils on a large shallow dish, garnished with fried onion slices, with the oil poured over.

This dish is delicious served either warm or cold, and accompanied by yoghourt.

- A tip: you may find it easier to cook rice and lentils separately and to mix them together when they are both done.
- For different flavours add 1 teaspoon cumin and 1 teaspoon coriander in the cooking water or 2 teaspoons dried mint.
- In another dish of rice and lentils called *masafi*, the lentils are turned to a purée. Red lentils, which disintegrate easily, can be used for this.

POTATOES WITH CHICK PEAS AND TOMATOES

This dish is eaten cold in the Middle East. The hot version is the same, except that it uses butter or *samna* (clarified butter) instead of oil.

> *1 kg (2 lb) potatoes*
> *3 onions, thickly sliced*
> *4–5 tablespoons oil*

60 g (2 oz) cooked chick peas
2–3 cloves garlic
500 g (1 lb) tomatoes, skinned and chopped
2 tablespoons tomato concentrate
Salt and black pepper

Peel and slice the potatoes thickly. Fry the onions in oil until golden, using a large saucepan. Add the chick peas and the whole garlic cloves, and fry until coloured. Add the potato slices and turn them until they too are slightly coloured. Add tomatoes, and water to cover mixed with tomato concentrate. Season to taste with salt and pepper.

Bring to the boil and simmer gently until the potatoes are done.

Serve cold.

OKRA (BAMIA) WITH TOMATOES AND ONIONS

This popular dish is often flavoured with garlic and coriander, a favourite Arab combination. It is customarily served cold, and for this reason it is cooked in oil. However, it is equally delicious hot, served with rice or as a side dish.

1 kg (2 lb) fresh young okra
375 g (12 oz) tiny white button onions or large onions
4–5 tablespoons olive oil
2–3 cloves garlic, halved
500 g (1 lb) tomatoes, skinned and sliced
Salt and black pepper
Juice of 1 lemon

Wash and scrub the fresh okra. Cut off any hard stems and dry them thoroughly. Peel the button onions but leave them whole. If using large onions, slice them thickly.

Heat the oil in a large saucepan and fry the onions with the halved garlic cloves until slightly soft, transparent and golden. Add okra and continue to fry until slightly softened. Add the sliced tomatoes and sauté for a few minutes longer. Season to taste with salt and pepper. Cover with water, bring to the boil and simmer until the okra are very tender, ½ to 1 hour. Squeeze in the lemon juice and cook for a further 15 minutes. (Tinned okra require a much shorter time.)

Serve hot or cold. If to be served cold, allow to cool in the saucepan before turning out into a serving dish.

• If you wish to flavour the dish with coriander, add 1 teaspoon of ground coriander together with the garlic cloves, which should in this case be crushed and not halved.

KOUSA BI GEBNA

Courgettes or Marrow with Cheese

A perfect vegetable dish. Although courgettes are traditionally used, marrow does very well. Use a good melting cheese such as Gruyère or Cheddar, mixed with a little Parmesan.

> *1 large onion, chopped*
> *2 tablespoons butter or oil*
> *1 kg (2 lb) courgettes or marrow*
> *Salt*
> *3 eggs*

250 g (8 oz) grated cheese
White pepper

Soften the onion in butter or oil. Wash the courgettes or marrow. Scrape skins lightly if necessary. Trim the courgette ends and cut into 1-cm (½-inch) slices. Cut the marrow into 3-cm (1-inch) cubes. Poach in salted water for a few minutes until tender, or steam if you prefer. Drain well. Put into an ovenproof dish and mix with the onions.

Beat the eggs, add the grated cheese and pepper to taste, and mix well. Pour over the vegetables.

Bake in a preheated moderate oven (180°C/350°F/Mark 4) for about 20 minutes. Allow the top to colour delicately.

Excellent served with yoghurt.

- Lately I have been adding a little grated nutmeg to the beaten eggs and found it very nice.

ALOO SFENAJ

Spinach and Prunes with Beans

A Persian combination.

120 g (4 oz) black-eyed beans or dried red beans
1 large onion, coarsely chopped
2–3 tablespoons oil
120 g (4 oz) pitted prunes
½ teaspoon turmeric
1 teaspoon cinnamon
Pepper

Salt
1 kg (2 lb) spinach

Soak the beans in water for an hour. Fry the onion in oil until golden in a large saucepan. Add the prunes and the drained beans, cover with water, add spices and pepper and cook until the beans are tender (from ½ to 1 hour) and the water much reduced, adding salt when the beans have softened. Wash the spinach and remove thick stems. Put it in the pan and cook, turning it over and stirring, for about 10 minutes until the spinach is done.

MASHED POTATOES WITH PINE NUTS

1 kg (2 lb) potatoes
2 tablespoons oil
1 large onion, coarsely chopped
3 tablespoons pine nuts
90 g (3 oz) butter
90 ml (3 fl oz) milk
Salt and pepper
1 teaspoon cinnamon
A good pinch of nutmeg
A good pinch of chilli pepper
1 tablespoon finely chopped parsley

Wash and boil the potatoes. Fry the onion in oil till golden, add the pine nuts and let them brown. Peel and mash the potatoes, beat in butter and milk and season with salt and pepper and spices. Serve with the onion and pine nuts on top and a sprinkling of parsley.

IMAM BAYILDI

'The Imam fainted'

This is a Turkish speciality. Widely conflicting stories are told about the origins of its name. Some say that the dish acquired it when an *imam* or Turkish priest fainted with pleasure on being served these stuffed aubergines by his wife. Others believe that the *imam* fainted when he heard how expensive the ingredients were, and how much olive oil had gone into the making of the dish.

The dish is delightful and, in fact, not very expensive. It makes a splendid first course.

> *6 long medium-sized aubergines*
> *Filling (see below)*
> *150 ml (¼ pint) olive oil*
> *1 teaspoon sugar, or more*
> *Salt*
> *Juice of 1 lemon*

Cut the aubergines in half lengthwise. They may be peeled or not, as you prefer. Scoop out the centres. Sprinkle the hollowed-out vegetables with salt, and leave to drain for at least half an hour. Then rinse with cold water and pat dry.

Fill each hollowed-out half with the following filling.

Filling

For vegetables prepared *à la Imam Bayildi*, to be eaten cold, and sometimes called *yalangi dolma* or 'false dolma', because of the lack of meat. A very popular filling in Turkey.

375 g (12 oz) onions
3–4 tablespoons olive oil
2–3 large cloves garlic, crushed
A bunch of parsley, finely chopped
375 g (12 oz) tomatoes, skinned, seeded and chopped
Salt

Slice the onions thinly. Soften them gently in olive oil, but do not let them colour. Add garlic and stir for a minute or two until aromatic. Remove from the heat and stir in parsley and tomatoes. Season to taste with salt, and mix well.

Arrange the stuffed aubergines side by side in a large pan. Pour over them the oil and enough water to cover (about 150 ml/ ¼ pint) mixed with a little sugar, salt to taste, and the lemon juice.

Cover the pan and simmer gently until the aubergines are very soft, about 1 hour. Remove from the heat and allow to cool. Turn into a serving dish. Serve cold.

• Substituting the water with tomato juice for cooking and adding 2 crushed cloves garlic adds to the taste.

HOW TO COOK RICE

Throughout the Middle East, the preparation of rice is enveloped by a certain ritual mystique. Although an extremely simple dish, various ways of cooking it exist. Each family cherishes a particular method and is sceptical about all others, refusing to believe that it is possible to achieve successful results in any way other than their own. Generally speaking however, each country seems to prefer one method above all others. I have given those most commonly followed.

Long-grain rice is used except for stuffing vegetables, when short- or medium-grain rice is preferred because it sticks together. The particular qualities of the longer grain lie in its fluffiness, and its ability to remain firm and separate. If well cooked, it is tender but firm, not too soft, and never mushy. Varieties of long-grain rice available in Britain include *basmati* and *patna* rice from India, and the American 'Uncle Ben'.

Basically, plain rice is cooked in water with salt and some fat – usually butter, clarified butter, oil or margarine. The quantity of water necessary and the cooking times vary. Each batch of rice is different and so, as households buy it by the large sackful, the first dish made from the opened sack ascertains the amount of water and the time required for cooking the rest. Generally the same volume of water as that of dry raw rice is needed, but if the rice is a year old more water must be used. It also depends on the type of grain.

The rice is almost always cooked in a pan with a tightly fitting lid, but a few people prefer to leave the lid only half on. In this case, more water must be used to make up for the rapid evaporation.

When rice comes in hessian sacks it has to be cleaned of stones and roughage (and sometimes small insects too) and washed many times before it is ready for cooking. The pre-packed rice available is perfectly clean and needs only to be rid of the starchy powder which causes it to be less separate and slightly sticky when cooked. Some people do not object to this and find the result of rice cooked without preliminary washing very acceptable, maintaining that the zeal of excessive washing is a hangover from the 'hessian sack' era.

A special word about Persian rice. As with her art of miniature painting and poetry, Persia has carried the preparation of rice to extraordinary heights of refinement. It is a base or accompaniment for practically every dish and it is said that no other Middle Eastern country prepares rice in the same perfectionist manner. Its preparation is often started a day before it is to be eaten.

At least six different qualities of rice are cultivated in Persia. The best, 'royal' rice, called *domsiah*, grows in rare conditions and is very expensive. The next best is *darbori* rice; then come *sadri* and *champâ*. These are not available in Britain. *Basmati* rice, now found in most supermarkets as well as in specialist shops, is the nearest to the third quality of rice and the best substitute to use.

WAYS OF COOKING PLAIN RICE

By some Middle Eastern standards 500 g (1 lb) of rice is needed to feed 2 people, but by European ones it is usually enough for 6. In my own family it satisfies 4.

It is more convenient to measure rice in teacupfuls because it is the accurate volume rather than the weight that is important in measuring the liquid for cooking. You will find that a large teacup, 225 ml (8 fl oz), holds about 250 g (8 oz) of rice.

In a few countries, though not all, it is considered preferable to cook the rice in stock. A chicken or meat stock left over from a soup or stew, used instead of water, will make a magnificent rice.

1. A Syrian Way

2 teacups long-grain rice
2 teacups water

Salt
60–90 g (2–3 oz) butter

To wash the rice, pour boiling water over it in a bowl and stir well for a few seconds. Pour into a sieve or a small-holed colander and rinse under cold running water until the water runs clear. Drain well.

Bring 2 cups water to the boil in a pan with a little salt to taste. Throw in the drained rice, bring to the boil again, and boil vigorously for 2 minutes. Cover the pan with a tight-fitting lid and simmer very gently, undisturbed, for about 20 minutes, until the water has been absorbed and the rice is cooked. It should be tender and separate, with little holes all over the surface. Turn off the heat, and allow the rice to rest for about 10 minutes.

Melt the butter (by today's standards this is rather a large quantity which you may prefer to reduce) in a saucepan and put it evenly all over the rice. Let it rest again, covered, for 3 minutes longer, until the melted fat has been absorbed by the rice.

2. A Lebanese Way

The ingredients and quantities are the same as above (although some people use half as much water).

Wash the rice as above and drain well. Put the 2 teacups water, salt and butter or margarine in a saucepan, and bring to the boil. Throw in the rice and boil vigorously for 2 minutes. Cover the pan tightly and simmer very gently, undisturbed, for about 20 minutes, until the rice is tender and fluffy, and little holes have appeared all over the surface. Turn off the heat and allow to rest for 10 minutes before serving.

3. An Egyptian Way

The ingredients and quantities are the same as in the first recipe, although Jewish households like my own used oil instead of butter.

Wash and drain the rice as above. Allow the rice grains to dry out as much as possible. (In this method the rice can be left unwashed if you wish.)

Heat the butter or oil in a saucepan. Throw in the rice and fry it gently for a minute or so, until the grains are translucent and well coated with fat. Add the water and salt to taste. Boil vigorously for 2 minutes, then simmer gently, tightly covered and undisturbed, for about 20 minutes, until the rice is tender and the characteristic little holes have appeared on the surface. Never stir while it is cooking. Allow to rest for 10 minutes before serving.

4. A Persian Way
and a particularly excellent one –
Chilau or Steamed Rice

Use *basmati* rice. Wash well in a colander then put it in a bowl with 2 tablespoons salt and lukewarm water to cover. Stir and let it soak overnight if you can, or for at least an hour. The longer the better.

Fill a large saucepan with plenty of water, add 2 tablespoons salt and bring to the boil. Sprinkle the drained rice in gradually and let it boil vigorously for about 4 to 8 minutes. The cooking time varies from one batch of rice to another and depends mainly on when it has been harvested. Test a grain of rice by biting it. When it is just a little underdone – it must be slightly harder than you would like to eat it – drain quickly and rinse in lukewarm water.

Put 2 tablespoons butter and let it melt at the bottom of the pan, then put in all the rice and stir. Cover with 2 more tablespoons butter. Stretch a clean dishcloth across the top of the pan, put the lid on top and lift the corners of the cloth up over it. (In Iran the lid, made of raffia and covered by a removable and washable cloth, is called a *damkoni*.)

Then leave the rice to steam over a very low flame for 20 to 30 minutes. It should be cooked and separate. The cloth will absorb the excess steam. The crisp, brown, golden crust that forms at the bottom is considered a delicacy to be offered first to guests. It is called *dig*. Remove it with a spatula and serve separately.

Some people like to put thin slices of fried bread or raw potato at the bottom of a pan when steaming with rice, and serve them in the same way as the crisp rice.

Although this preparation may sound complicated, it is not so, and the result is so exquisite that it is well worth trying. You will understand the importance of rice in Persian life and the national pride in making it to perfection.

Chilau can be eaten with a generous lump of butter and, traditionally, with a raw egg yolk served in an egg-shell. The yolk is poured over each individual portion of rice and then stirred into it, making a glistening creamy sauce.

RICE WITH DATES AND ALMONDS

An Arab dish, said to be of Bedouin origin.

> 2 *teacups* (*500 g/1 lb*) *long-grain rice*
> Salt

120 g (4 oz) blanched almonds, halved
120 g (4 oz) butter
60 g (2 oz) raisins
*120 g (4 oz) dates, chopped (dried dates will do, if soft
   and juicy)*

Wash and boil the rice until not quite tender, following the recipe for *chilau* (page 50). Drain and keep warm.

Fry the almonds in 60 g (2 oz) butter until just golden. Add raisins and dates, and stir gently over moderate heat for a few minutes longer. Add about ¾ teacup water and simmer gently for a further 15 minutes until the dates are soft and the water has been absorbed.

Melt a tablespoon of butter in a large, heavy saucepan. Add half of the rice and spread evenly with the date and almond mixture. Cover with the remaining rice and dot the top with butter shavings. Cover with a clean cloth and tight-fitting lid, and steam over very low heat for about 30 minutes.

TOMATO PILAV

250 g (8 oz) onions, chopped
3 tablespoons nut or olive oil
1 clove garlic (optional)
*750 g–1 kg (1½–2 lb) ripe tomatoes, skinned, or a 850-g
   (30-oz) tin skinned tomatoes*
Salt and black pepper
1 teaspoon sugar (optional)
1 bay leaf (optional)
1 teaspoon dried oregano (optional)

2 teacups (500 g/1 lb) long-grain rice, washed and
  drained

In a large, heavy saucepan, fry the onions in hot oil until soft and golden. A whole clove of garlic may be added to the onions if liked. Add the tomatoes and season to taste with salt, pepper, and a little sugar if needed. Sauté lightly, squashing the tomatoes a little with a fork, until they acquire a 'fried' taste. Cover with water and allow to simmer gently for about ¾ hour. This sauce may be perfumed with a bay leaf or oregano, but it is also good plain. Add more water while cooking if required.

When the sauce has become rich in flavour and texture, throw in the rice. Add a little water to the pan to make up the liquid to about the same volume as that of the rice. Bring to the boil and simmer gently, covered and undisturbed, for about 20 minutes, until the rice is tender. It will have acquired a pale, salmon pink colour and will be impregnated with the flavour of the tomatoes.

ISABEL ALLENDE · *Voices in My Ear*

NICHOLSON BAKER · *Playing Trombone*

LINDSEY BAREHAM · *The Little Book of Big Soups*

KAREN BLIXEN · *From the Ngong Hills*

DIRK BOGARDE · *Coming of Age*

ANTHONY BURGESS · *Childhood*

ANGELA CARTER · *Lizzie Borden*

CARLOS CASTANEDA · *The Sorcerer's Ring of Power*

ELIZABETH DAVID · *Peperonata and Other Italian Dishes*

RICHARD DAWKINS · *The Pocket Watchmaker*

GERALD DURRELL · *The Pageant of Fireflies*

RICHARD ELLMANN · *The Trial of Oscar Wilde*

EPICURUS · *Letter on Happiness*

MARIANNE FAITHFULL · *Year One*

KEITH FLOYD · *Hot and Spicy Floyd*

ALEXANDER FRATER · *Where the Dawn Comes Up Like Thunder*

ESTHER FREUD · *Meeting Bilal*

JOHN KENNETH GALBRAITH · *The Culture of Contentment*

ROB GRANT AND DOUG NAYLOR · *Scenes from the Dwarf*

ROBERT GRAVES · *The Gods of Olympus*

JANE GRIGSON · *Puddings*

SOPHIE GRIGSON · *From Sophie's Table*

KATHARINE HEPBURN · *Little Me*

SUSAN HILL · *The Badness Within Him*

ALAN HOLLINGHURST · *Adventures Underground*

BARRY HUMPHRIES · *Less is More Please*

HOWARD JACOBSON · *Expulsion from Paradise*

P. D. JAMES · *The Girl Who Loved Graveyards*

STEPHEN KING · *Umney's Last Case*

LAO TZU · *Tao Te Ching*

DAVID LEAVITT · *Chips Is Here*

PENGUIN 60s

LAURIE LEE · *To War in Spain*

PATRICK LEIGH FERMOR · *Loose as the Wind*

ELMORE LEONARD · *Trouble at Rindo's Station*

DAVID LODGE · *Surprised by Summer*

BERNARD MAC LAVERTY · *The Miraculous Candidate*

SHENA MACKAY · *Cloud-Cuckoo-Land*

NORMAN MAILER · *The Dressing Room*

PETER MAYLE · *Postcards from Summer*

JAN MORRIS · *Scenes from Havian Life*

BLAKE MORRISON · *Camp Cuba*

VLADIMIR NABOKOV · *Now Remember*

REDMOND O'HANLON · *A River in Borneo*

STEVEN PINKER · *Thinking in Tongues*

CRAIG RAINE · *Private View*

CLAUDIA RODEN · *Ful Medames and Other Vegetarian Dishes*

HELGE RUBINSTEIN · *Chocolate Parfait*

SIMON SCHAMA · *The Taking of the Bastille*

WILL SELF · *The Rock of Crack As Big As the Ritz*

MARK SHAND · *Elephant Tales*

NIGEL SLATER · *30-Minute Suppers*

RICK STEIN · *Fresh from the Sea*

LYTTON STRACHEY · *Florence Nightingale*

PAUL THEROUX · *Slow Trains to Simla*

COLIN THUBRON · *Samarkand*

MARK TULLY · *Beyond Purdah*

LAURENS VAN DER POST · *Merry Christmas, Mr Lawrence*

MARGARET VISSER · *More than Meets the Eye*

GAVIN YOUNG · *Something of Samoa*

and

Thirty Obituaries from Wisden · SELECTED BY MATTHEW ENGEL

READ MORE IN PENGUIN

For complete information about books available from Penguin and how to order them, please write to us at the appropriate address below. Please note that for copyright reasons the selection of books varies from country to country.

IN THE UNITED KINGDOM: Please write to *Dept. EP, Penguin Books Ltd, Bath Road, Harmondsworth, Middlesex UB7 0DA.*

IN THE UNITED STATES: Please write to *Consumer Sales, Penguin USA, P.O. Box 999, Dept. 17109, Bergenfield, New Jersey 07621-0120.* VISA and MasterCard holders call 1-800-253-6476 to order Penguin titles.

IN CANADA: Please write to *Penguin Books Canada Ltd, 10 Alcorn Avenue, Suite 300, Toronto, Ontario M4V 3B2.*

IN AUSTRALIA: Please write to *Penguin Books Australia Ltd, P.O. Box 257, Ringwood, Victoria 3134.*

IN NEW ZEALAND: Please write to *Penguin Books (NZ) Ltd, Private Bag 102902, North Shore Mail Centre, Auckland 10.*

IN INDIA: Please write to *Penguin Books India Pvt Ltd, 706 Eros Apartments, 56 Nehru Place, New Delhi 110 019.*

IN THE NETHERLANDS: Please write to *Penguin Books Netherlands bv, Postbus 3507, NL-1001 AH Amsterdam.*

IN GERMANY: Please write to *Penguin Books Deutschland GmbH, Metzlerstrasse 26, 60594 Frankfurt am Main.*

IN SPAIN: Please write to *Penguin Books S. A., Bravo Murillo 19, 1º B, 28015 Madrid.*

IN ITALY: Please write to *Penguin Italia s.r.l., Via Felice Casati 20, I-20124 Milano.*

IN FRANCE: Please write to *Penguin France S. A., 17 rue Lejeune, F-31000 Toulouse.*

IN JAPAN: Please write to *Penguin Books Japan, Ishikiribashi Building, 2-5-4, Suido, Bunkyo-ku, Tokyo 112.*

IN GREECE: Please write to *Penguin Hellas Ltd, Dimocritou 3, GR-106 71 Athens.*

IN SOUTH AFRICA: Please write to *Longman Penguin Southern Africa (Pty) Ltd, Private Bag X08, Bertsham 2013.*